THE SCHIZOAFFECTIVE WORKBOOK

Create Your Own Plan to Eliminate Schizoaffective Effects, Therapeutic Journal Adapted from Cognitive and Dialectical Behavioral Therapy for Bipolar Type.

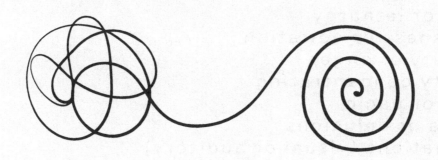

BY
MESLOUB IHEB

SZA - MOOD SWINGS
WORKSHEET

Date: _____

Mood rating (1-10 scale):
 1 = extremely sad, hopeless, or depressed
 5 = neither happy nor sad, neutral
 10 = extremely happy, excited, or elated

Time of day: _____

Mood description (describe the mood in your own words):

Possible triggers (what events or situations may have caused the mood change):

Symptoms (check all that apply):

__ Racing thoughts
__ Fatigue or lethargy
__ Restlessness or agitation
__ Irritability or anger
__ Difficulty concentrating
__ Anxiety or panic
__ Paranoia or delusions
__ Hallucinations (visual or auditory)
__ Difficulty sleeping
__ Appetite changes
__ Physical symptoms:(e.g. headache, stomachache, etc.)

Coping strategies: (what did you do to manage the mood swing?)

SZA - MOOD SWINGS WORKSHEET

Date: _____

Mood rating (1-10 scale):
 1 = extremely sad, hopeless, or depressed
 5 = neither happy nor sad, neutral
 10 = extremely happy, excited, or elated

Time of day: _____

Mood description (describe the mood in your own words):

_____

Possible triggers (what events or situations may have caused the mood change):

_____

Symptoms (check all that apply):

__ Racing thoughts
__ Fatigue or lethargy
__ Restlessness or agitation
__ Irritability or anger
__ Difficulty concentrating
__ Anxiety or panic
__ Paranoia or delusions
__ Hallucinations (visual or auditory)
__ Difficulty sleeping
__ Appetite changes
__ Physical symptoms:(e.g. headache, stomachache, etc.)

Coping strategies: (what did you do to manage the mood swing?)

_____

_____

_____

SZA - MOOD SWINGS WORKSHEET

Date: _____

Mood rating (1-10 scale):
 1 = extremely sad, hopeless, or depressed
 5 = neither happy nor sad, neutral
 10 = extremely happy, excited, or elated

Time of day: _____

Mood description (describe the mood in your own words):

Possible triggers (what events or situations may have caused the mood change):

Symptoms (check all that apply):

--
--
--
--
--
__ Physical symptoms:
--
--
--
--

Coping strategies: (what did you do to manage the mood swing?)

SZA - MOOD SWINGS
WORKSHEET

Date: _____

Mood rating (1-10 scale):
 1 = extremely sad, hopeless, or depressed
 5 = neither happy nor sad, neutral
 10 = extremely happy, excited, or elated

Time of day: _____

Mood description (describe the mood in your own words):

Possible triggers (what events or situations may have
caused the mood change):

Symptoms (check all that apply):

 --
 --
 --
 --
 --
 __ Physical symptoms:
 --
 --
 --
 --

Coping strategies: (what did you do to manage the mood
swing?)

SCHIZOAFFECTIVE
MOOD SWINGS WORKSHEET

Date: _____

Mood rating (1-10 scale):
 1 = extremely sad, hopeless, or depressed
 5 = neither happy nor sad, neutral
 10 = extremely happy, excited, or elated

Time of day: _____

Mood description (describe the mood in your own words):

Possible triggers (what events or situations may have caused the mood change):

Symptoms (check all that apply):

__ Racing thoughts
__ Fatigue or lethargy
__ Restlessness or agitation
__ Irritability or anger
__ Difficulty concentrating
__ Anxiety or panic
__ Paranoia or delusions
__ Hallucinations (visual or auditory)
__ Difficulty sleeping
__ Appetite changes
__ Physical symptoms:(e.g. headache, stomachache, etc.)

Coping strategies: (what did you do to manage the mood swing?)

ANXIETY WORKSHEET

The way you think has an impact on how you feel. Anxiety might cause you to exaggerate the risk of a situation while underestimating your capacity to deal with it. Rather than leaping to the worst-case scenario in a circumstance that makes you uneasy, try to think of various interpretations. Examine the evidence for and against your hypothesis.

DELUSIONS WORKSHEET

Determine whether your delusions are related to specific events or behaviors, or whether they occur at a specific time of day due to a flare-up of your schizophrenic symptoms. This can help you identify conditions that may trigger your diving into delusions. Some delusions are brief and fleeting, while others are The other is more stable and they stay for a long time.

_____

_____

_____

_____

_____

_____

_____

_____

_____

_____

_____

_____

_____

_____

_____

_____

_____

_____

_____

_____

_____

_____

SUICIDAL THOUGHTS

Remember that the soul is something dear in this world. God created life for it. On this piece of paper, write a pledge to yourself that you will not do anything that will harm you in the future and that you will resist all destructive obsessions that motivate you to do this thing.

Set appropriate urgent measures that you can resort to if these thoughts attack you. You must realize that these thoughts are nothing but an imaginary enemy. You are in a battle to recover from this disorder. You must win this battle no matter what it costs you.

HALLUCINATIONS - SZA

Instructions: *Try to find explanations for the following questions to help you deal with hallucinations.*

- *Determine the moral reasons or situations that make you hallucinating?*
- *How often do you experience hallucinations? What is the nature of your hallucinations? (What do you hear, see, or feel?)*
- *What do you usually do when you experience these disturbing hallucinations? (Example: Are you trying to ignore her, how do you deal with her?)*

- *Classify and rate the coping techniques you have used in the past to deal with hallucinations? Useful and not useful?*
- *What new coping strategies would you like to try and what resources are available to you for additional support to manage hallucinations?*

HALLUCINATIONS

HALLUCINATIONS - SZA

- *Find out and write down the coping strategies that work best for you. This may include:*
- *deep breathing exercises (a model to experiment with when you feel hallucinations approaching try to focus directly on your breath and the physical sensation of breathing look around the room and name the things you see try at the same time to engage your senses, such as smelling a strong smell or holding something with a distinctive texture),*
- *Add distraction techniques such as reading, talking to a close friend, or making positive contact with a family member.*

HALLUCINATIONS

RELATIONSHIP AND SCHIZOAFFECTIVE DISORDER

Title: Understanding the Paradoxes of the Relationship with Schizoaffective Disorder

Instructions:
- Try to explore how schizoaffective disorder affects your relationships and explore tools to promote healthy relationships.

Step 1:
- Try to accurately identify the schizoaffective symptoms affecting relationships.
- List the symptoms that most affect your relationships (eg, sudden mood swings, social isolation, paranoia, etc.).

Step 2:
- Explore negative relationship patterns
- Reflect on a past relationship and identify any negative patterns in that relationship. like :
*Avoidance of social situations due to anxiety or fear of judgment
*Excessive clinging to a partner
*Difficulty expressing emotional needs and feelings effectively

Step 3:
Select Trigger Styles
Think about situations that trigger symptoms of schizoaffective disorder. Examples may include:

-*Bad or impactful events (such as job loss, bankruptcy or financial stress, severe illness)*
-*Social situations (such as parties or places that are associated with certain feelings)*
-*Misunderstanding in relationships*

RELATIONSHIP AND SCHIZOAFFECTIVE DISORDER

RELATIONSHIP AND SCHIZOAFFECTIVE DISORDER

HEALTHY COMMUNICATION IN RELATIONSHIPS

Instructions:

Think about the communication skills of your relationships and identify areas to work on.

- How do you express your thoughts and feelings to others? Do you achieve the required psychological satisfaction?
- Are you an active listener? Do I listen to understand, or do I listen to answer?
- Do I have the ability to communicate my needs and limits effectively to the other party?
- Do I express myself firmly or do I fear confrontation face to face?

HEALTHY COMMUNICATION IN RELATIONSHIPS

ISOLATION WORKSHEET

Think carefully about reconstructing positive patterns of your thinking about isolation:

Identifying isolation triggers: Highlight situations or experiences that trigger your feelings of isolation. Examples may include:

- *I prefer to be isolated a lot*
- *Others always misunderstand me*
- *I avoid engaging in certain activities for fear of rejection or negative criticism.*

Recognizing thoughts of isolation: Determine what thoughts go through your mind when you want to be isolated. These thoughts are often irrational or self-defeating. some examples :

- *"I feel like a burden to others."*
- *"I just don't have the skills to be around other people."*

Challenging isolating thoughts: Once you have identified a framework for your isolating thoughts, it is necessary to challenge them according to specific therapeutic mechanisms. Ask yourself the following questions:

- *Are these ideas based on logical facts, are they useful to me, or are they just false beliefs?*
- *Are there any real explanations for these ideas?*
- *How would I react if a friend I know had these thoughts? What advice would I give him about solitude?*

The stage of changing negative thoughts into positive thoughts: At this point, focus only on positive self-talk. Follow the following examples that you can rely on:

- *No one is perfect, but I have the capabilities to impress anyone with my presence.*
- *"Despite the emotional damage I'm going through, I have amazing people around me in my life."*
- *"I deserve satisfactory relationships for my life, I can contribute to any relationship I enter into because I have the intellectual ingredients and I can make the other party feel that he deserves me because I ...."*
- *"I am worthy of love and respect because I possess the following positive qualities: ...."*

ISOLATION WORKSHEET

ISOLATION WORKSHEET

DISORGANIZED THINKING AND SPEECH

Instructions:
Disorganized thinking and speech are obstacles to communicating effectively with others and expressing ideas clearly.
This worksheet will help you learn to organize your thoughts and improve your communication skills with others.

Step 1: Determine the main point of your target topic.
- *Think about what you want to convey in your speech and carefully select the focal point you want to make.*
Try to think about it carefully and write it down in one sentence.

Example: I want to tell my husband about my anxiety and how it affects my daily life.

Step 2: Supporting the main point (brainstorm)
After you are able to identify the main point, provide a set of supporting points that will help you clarify the main point.
Example:
- *Explain how anxiety affected your focus.*
- *Describe how your anxiety reflects in social situations and how it affects your daily life.*
- *Among these reflections, we find, for example, excessive thinking and the problem of sleep.*

Step 3: Organize your thoughts and practice effective communication
- *Practice accurately communicating your main point. Try to arrange your ideas. You can practice with a friend or family member. Try to avoid random, irrelevant thoughts.*
Example :
- *Anxiety affected my social performance, so I lost focus in various conversations, which makes me speak illogically, homogeneously, and lack a compass.*
- *I always suspect that the anxiety I have is also associated with social anxiety because my loss of focus is preceded by some tension due to my fear of social situations..This has been reflected in the quality of my life and my sleep at night...I have become a mass of fatigue because of that...*

Step 4:Evaluate your connections
After you have practiced your structured communication, continue to assess your performance. Did you really pass your key point effectively? Have you explained your main view and associated supporting ideas clearly? Were you able to avoid going off topic?
.

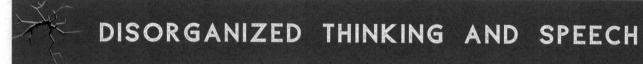

DISORGANIZED THINKING AND SPEECH

REVERSING S.Z.A SYMPTOMS WORKSHEET

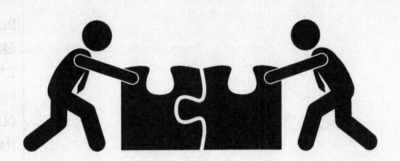

Exposure Therapy
Scheme for
Schizoaffective
Symptoms

Self-Therapy

SCHIZOAFFECTIVE DISORDER
DBT WORKSHEET

TRACK PSYCHOLOGICAL AND EMOTIONAL ISSUES RELATED TO UNUSUAL
FEELINGS, PERCEPTIONS, AND ACTIONS
YOUR PROBLEMS MANAGING DAILY LIFE ACTIVITIES OR ANY DISORGANIZED
THOUGHTS DUE TO LACK OF MOTIVATION OR EMOTIONAL DRYNESS...
YOUR EMOTIONAL PROBLEMS COPING WITH CHALLENGES AT WORK, OR
HOME.

✓ __ : __

_____

_____

_____

_____

✓ __ : __

_____

_____

_____

_____

✓ __ : __

_____

_____

_____

_____

A DAILY WIN

_____

_____

_____

_____

Daily Mood Checker ✓

Mood	
ANGRY	☐
ANNOYED	☐
ANXIOUS	☐
ASHAMED	☐
AWKWARD	☐
BRAVE	☐
CALM	☐
CHEERFUL	☐
CHILL	☐
CONFUSED	☐
DISCOURAGED	☐
DISTRACTED	☐
EMBARRASSED	☐
EXCITED	☐
FRIENDLY	☐
GUILTY	☐
HAPPY	☐
HOPEFUL	☐
LONELY	☐
LOVED	☐
NERVOUS	☐
OFFENDED	☐
SCARED	☐
THOUGHTFUL	☐
TIRED	☐
UNCOMFORTABLE	☐
UNSURE	☐

DATE :   /   /

SELF-EXPOSURE
THERAPY
FOR SZA-BIPOLAR TRAITS

As part of your daily life, try to avoid situations that trigger symptoms of bipolar disorder and depression, as well as your feelings and mood swings.
But if the opposite happens, try to explore your inner triggers and contradictions in order to better understand your condition.

ALL ABOUT PSYCHOTIC AND MANIC TRIGGERS :	Notes :
	◯ ◯ ◯ ◯ ◯
ALL ABOUT DEPRESSIVE TRIGGERS :	Notes :
	◯ ◯ ◯ ◯ ◯
ALL ABOUT MOOD SWINGS TRIGGERS :	Notes :
	◯ ◯ ◯ ◯ ◯

Notes

....

....

OVERCOMING SZA
COPING SKILLS WORKSHEET

> Through this table, here are some of the problems that the majority of those suffering from schizoaffective disorder suffer from. Try to identify the difficulties associated with the items listed in the table. Try to find field solutions for them in reality, and then evaluate your progress each time.

• solving problems • forming relationships • learning useful behaviors • learn new skills	situations you exposed to and coping skills used
	👍 **WHAT WAS SO COOL:** ✋ **WHAT WASN'T COOL:**

CHALLENGING S.Z.A SYMPTOMS DBT WORKSHEET

Date : ....

OPEN CHALLENGE

Try to develop short or long-term plans to improve the quality of your life, in which you discuss the following:

- Your Strategies to develop a support network of family , friend, and healthcare professionals to help you stay well.
- What steps can you take to manage future episodes ?
- Your ways to fix emotional , behavioral , physical changes, do you notice when you are becoming symptomatic.
- Your self-care activities and self-talk affirmations that you practice on a daily basis to improve your mood and emotional and mental health.
- Discuss anything related to your mental health, social status, and all your internal contradictions

_____

_____

_____

_____

_____

_____

_____

_____

_____

_____

_____

_____

_____

_____

_____

S.Z.A MOOD CYCLE

Instructions: Think about your day from start to finish. Color the first square to express your feelings each time of the day. Next, write a word that reflects your feelings, and draw in the circle a picture of your face that reflects your feelings at that moment.

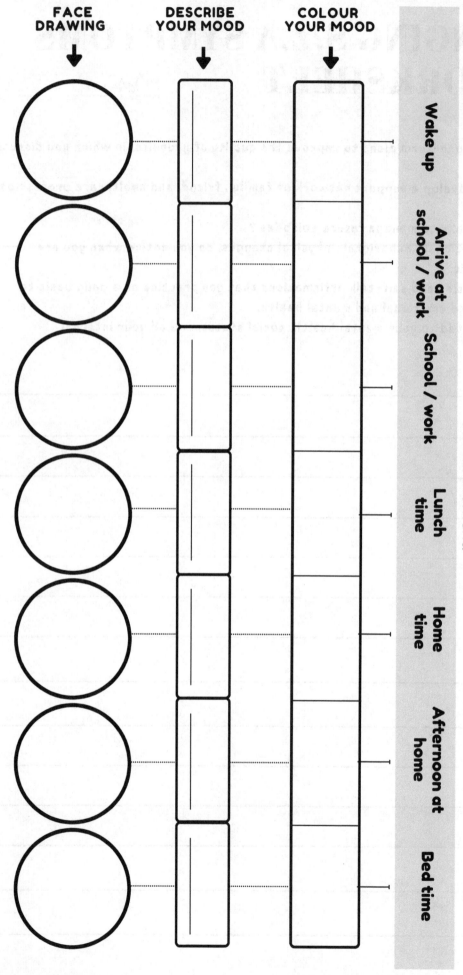

FACE DRAWING

DESCRIBE YOUR MOOD

COLOUR YOUR MOOD

Wake up

Arrive at school / work

School / work

Lunch time

Home time

Afternoon at home

Bed time

SCHIZOAFFECTIVE DISORDER
DBT WORKSHEET

TRACK PSYCHOLOGICAL AND EMOTIONAL ISSUES RELATED TO UNUSUAL
FEELINGS, PERCEPTIONS, AND ACTIONS
YOUR PROBLEMS MANAGING DAILY LIFE ACTIVITIES OR ANY DISORGANIZED
THOUGHTS DUE TO LACK OF MOTIVATION OR EMOTIONAL DRYNESS...
YOUR EMOTIONAL PROBLEMS COPING WITH CHALLENGES AT WORK, OR
HOME.

✓ ___ : ___

_____

_____

_____

✓ ___ : ___

_____

_____

_____

_____

✓ ___ : ___

_____

_____

_____

Daily Mood Checker ✓

Mood	
ANGRY	☐
ANNOYED	☐
ANXIOUS	☐
ASHAMED	☐
AWKWARD	☐
BRAVE	☐
CALM	☐
CHEERFUL	☐
CHILL	☐
CONFUSED	☐
DISCOURAGED	☐
DISTRACTED	☐
EMBARRASSED	☐
EXCITED	☐
FRIENDLY	☐
GUILTY	☐
HAPPY	☐
HOPEFUL	☐
LONELY	☐
LOVED	☐
NERVOUS	☐
OFFENDED	☐
SCARED	☐
THOUGHTFUL	☐
TIRED	☐
UNCOMFORTABLE	☐
UNSURE	☐

A DAILY WIN

_____

_____

_____

_____

SELF-EXPOSURE THERAPY FOR SZA-BIPOLAR TRAITS

As part of your daily life, try to avoid situations that trigger symptoms of bipolar disorder and depression, as well as your feelings and mood swings.
But if the opposite happens, try to explore your inner triggers and contradictions in order to better understand your condition.

ALL ABOUT PSYCHOTIC AND MANIC TRIGGERS :	Notes :
	○ ○ ○ ○ ○
ALL ABOUT DEPRESSIVE TRIGGERS :	Notes :
	○ ○ ○ ○ ○
ALL ABOUT MOOD SWINGS TRIGGERS :	Notes :
	○ ○ ○ ○ ○

Notes

....

....

OVERCOMING SZA
COPING SKILLS WORKSHEET

Through this table, here are some of the problems that the majority of those suffering from schizoaffective disorder suffer from. Try to identify the difficulties associated with the items listed in the table. Try to find field solutions for them in reality, and then evaluate your progress each time.

• solving problems • forming relationships • learning useful behaviors • learn new skills	situations you exposed to and coping skills used
	👍 **WHAT WAS SO COOL:** ✋ **WHAT WASN'T COOL:**

CHALLENGING S.Z.A SYMPTOMS DBT WORKSHEET

Date : ....

OPEN CHALLENGE

Try to develop short or long-term plans to improve the quality of your life, in which you discuss the following:

- Your Strategies to develop a support network of family , friend, and healthcare professionals to help you stay well.
- What steps can you take to manage future episodes ?
- Your ways to fix emotional , behavioral , physical changes, do you notice when you are becoming symptomatic.
- Your self-care activities and self-talk affirmations that you practice on a daily basis to improve your mood and emotional and mental health.
- Discuss anything related to your mental health, social status, and all your internal contradictions

_____

_____

_____

_____

_____

_____

_____

_____

_____

_____

_____

_____

S.Z.A MOOD CYCLE

Instructions: Think about your day from start to finish. Color the first square to express your feelings each time of the day. Next, write a word that reflects your feelings, and draw in the circle a picture of your face that reflects your feelings at that moment.

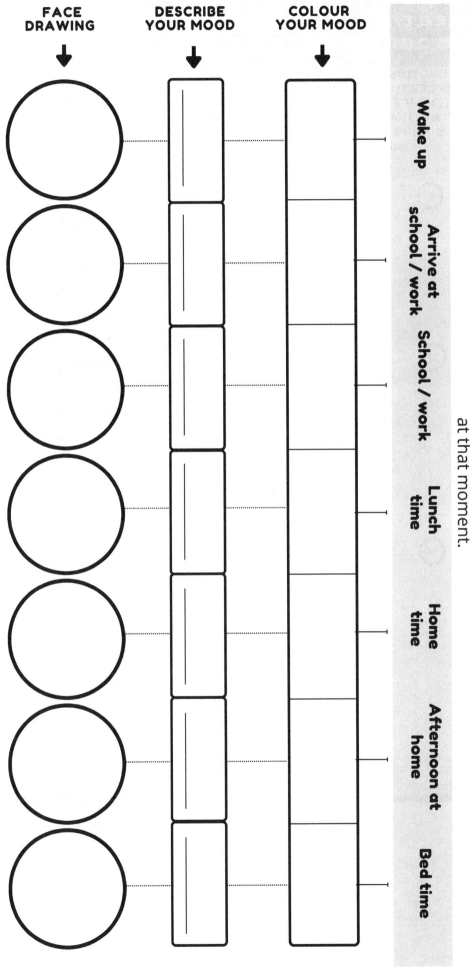

FACE DRAWING

DESCRIBE YOUR MOOD

COLOUR YOUR MOOD

Wake up

Arrive at school / work

School / work

Lunch time

Home time

Afternoon at home

Bed time

SCHIZOAFFECTIVE DISORDER
DBT WORKSHEET

Date : / /

Sleep quality :

TRACK PSYCHOLOGICAL AND EMOTIONAL ISSUES RELATED TO UNUSUAL FEELINGS, PERCEPTIONS, AND ACTIONS
YOUR PROBLEMS MANAGING DAILY LIFE ACTIVITIES OR ANY DISORGANIZED THOUGHTS DUE TO LACK OF MOTIVATION OR EMOTIONAL DRYNESS...
YOUR EMOTIONAL PROBLEMS COPING WITH CHALLENGES AT WORK, OR HOME.

✓ __ : __

_____
_____
_____

✓ __ : __

_____
_____
_____

✓ __ : __

_____
_____
_____

A DAILY WIN

_____
_____
_____
_____

Daily Mood Checker ✓

Mood	
ANGRY	☐
ANNOYED	☐
ANXIOUS	☐
ASHAMED	☐
AWKWARD	☐
BRAVE	☐
CALM	☐
CHEERFUL	☐
CHILL	☐
CONFUSED	☐
DISCOURAGED	☐
DISTRACTED	☐
EMBARRASSED	☐
EXCITED	☐
FRIENDLY	☐
GUILTY	☐
HAPPY	☐
HOPEFUL	☐
LONELY	☐
LOVED	☐
NERVOUS	☐
OFFENDED	☐
SCARED	☐
THOUGHTFUL	☐
TIRED	☐
UNCOMFORTABLE	☐
UNSURE	☐

DATE :   /   /

SELF-EXPOSURE THERAPY
FOR SZA-BIPOLAR TRAITS

As part of your daily life, try to avoid situations that trigger symptoms of bipolar disorder and depression, as well as your feelings and mood swings.
But if the opposite happens, try to explore your inner triggers and contradictions in order to better understand your condition.

ALL ABOUT PSYCHOTIC AND MANIC TRIGGERS :	Notes :
	○ ○ ○ ○ ○
ALL ABOUT DEPRESSIVE TRIGGERS :	Notes :
	○ ○ ○ ○ ○
ALL ABOUT MOOD SWINGS TRIGGERS :	Notes :
	○ ○ ○ ○ ○

Notes

....

....

OVERCOMING SZA
COPING SKILLS WORKSHEET

Through this table, here are some of the problems that the majority of those suffering from schizoaffective disorder suffer from. Try to identify the difficulties associated with the items listed in the table. Try to find field solutions for them in reality, and then evaluate your progress each time.

• solving problems • forming relationships • learning useful behaviors • learn new skills	situations you exposed to and coping skills used
	👍 WHAT WAS SO COOL: 🖐 WHAT WASN'T COOL:

CHALLENGING S.Z.A SYMPTOMS DBT WORKSHEET

Date : ....

OPEN CHALLENGE

Try to develop short or long-term plans to improve the quality of your life, in which you discuss the following:

- Your Strategies to develop a support network of family , friend, and healthcare professionals to help you stay well.
- What steps can you take to manage future episodes ?
- Your ways to fix emotional , behavioral , physical changes, do you notice when you are becoming symptomatic.
- Your self-care activities and self-talk affirmations that you practice on a daily basis to improve your mood and emotional and mental health.
- Discuss anything related to your mental health, social status, and all your internal contradictions

_____

_____

_____

_____

_____

_____

_____

_____

_____

_____

_____

_____

S.Z.A MOOD CYCLE

Instructions: Think about your day from start to finish. Color the first square to express your feelings each time of the day. Next, write a word that reflects your feelings, and draw in the circle a picture of your face that reflects your feelings at that moment.

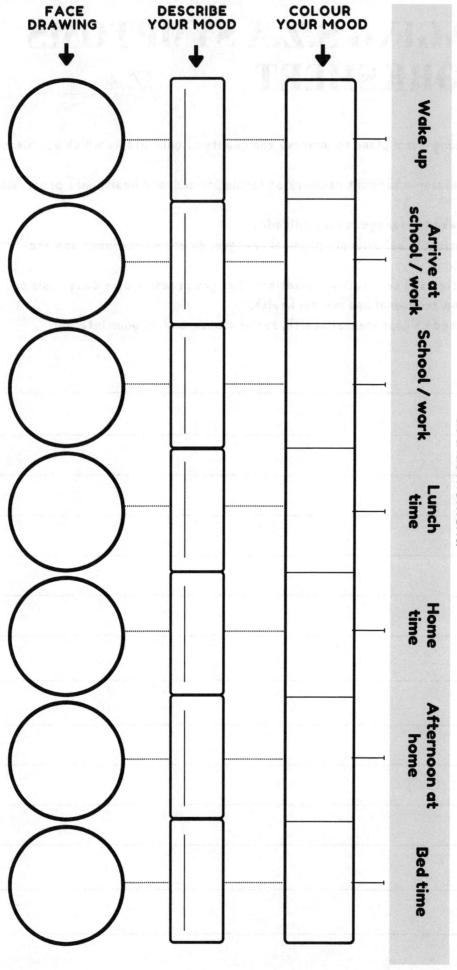

FACE DRAWING

DESCRIBE YOUR MOOD

COLOUR YOUR MOOD

Wake up

Arrive at school / work

School / work

Lunch time

Home time

Afternoon at home

Bed time

SCHIZOAFFECTIVE DISORDER
DBT WORKSHEET

Date : / /

Sleep quality :

TRACK PSYCHOLOGICAL AND EMOTIONAL ISSUES RELATED TO UNUSUAL
FEELINGS, PERCEPTIONS, AND ACTIONS
YOUR PROBLEMS MANAGING DAILY LIFE ACTIVITIES OR ANY DISORGANIZED
THOUGHTS DUE TO LACK OF MOTIVATION OR EMOTIONAL DRYNESS...
YOUR EMOTIONAL PROBLEMS COPING WITH CHALLENGES AT WORK, OR
HOME.

✓ ___ : ___

✓ ___ : ___

✓ ___ : ___

A DAILY WIN

Daily Mood Checker ✓

ANGRY	☐
ANNOYED	☐
ANXIOUS	☐
ASHAMED	☐
AWKWARD	☐
BRAVE	☐
CALM	☐
CHEERFUL	☐
CHILL	☐
CONFUSED	☐
DISCOURAGED	☐
DISTRACTED	☐
EMBARRASSED	☐
EXCITED	☐
FRIENDLY	☐
GUILTY	☐
HAPPY	☐
HOPEFUL	☐
LONELY	☐
LOVED	☐
NERVOUS	☐
OFFENDED	☐
SCARED	☐
THOUGHTFUL	☐
TIRED	☐
UNCOMFORTABLE	☐
UNSURE	☐

SELF-EXPOSURE THERAPY FOR SZA-BIPOLAR TRAITS

As part of your daily life, try to avoid situations that trigger symptoms of bipolar disorder and depression, as well as your feelings and mood swings.

But if the opposite happens, try to explore your inner triggers and contradictions in order to better understand your condition.

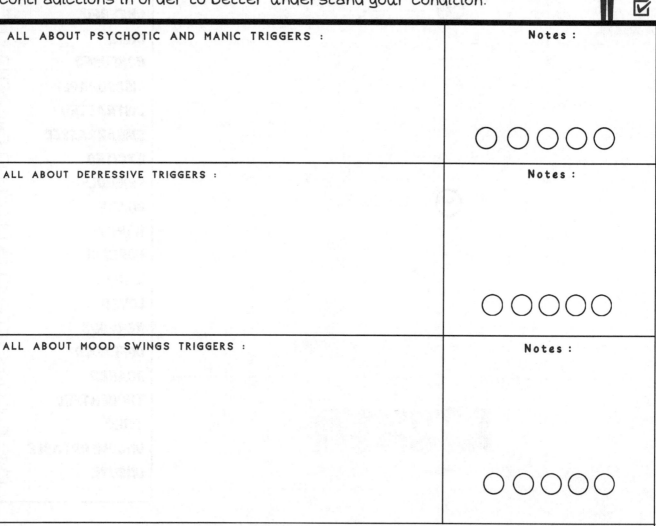

ALL ABOUT PSYCHOTIC AND MANIC TRIGGERS :	Notes :
	○ ○ ○ ○ ○
ALL ABOUT DEPRESSIVE TRIGGERS :	Notes :
	○ ○ ○ ○ ○
ALL ABOUT MOOD SWINGS TRIGGERS :	Notes :
	○ ○ ○ ○ ○

Notes

....

....

OVERCOMING SZA
COPING SKILLS WORKSHEET

Through this table, here are some of the problems that the majority of those suffering from schizoaffective disorder suffer from. Try to identify the difficulties associated with the items listed in the table. Try to find field solutions for them in reality, and then evaluate your progress each time.

• solving problems • forming relationships • learning useful behaviors • learn new skills	situations you exposed to and coping skills used
	👍 **WHAT WAS SO COOL:** ✋ **WHAT WASN'T COOL:**

CHALLENGING S.Z.A SYMPTOMS DBT WORKSHEET

Date : ....

OPEN CHALLENGE

Try to develop short or long-term plans to improve the quality of your life, in which you discuss the following:

- Your Strategies to develop a support network of family , friend, and healthcare professionals to help you stay well.
- What steps can you take to manage future episodes ?
- Your ways to fix emotional , behavioral , physical changes, do you notice when you are becoming symptomatic.
- Your self-care activities and self-talk affirmations that you practice on a daily basis to improve your mood and emotional and mental health.
- Discuss anything related to your mental health, social status, and all your internal contradictions

_____

_____

_____

_____

_____

_____

_____

_____

_____

_____

_____

_____

_____

S.Z.A MOOD CYCLE

Instructions: Think about your day from start to finish. Color the first square to express your feelings each time of the day. Next, write a word that reflects your feelings, and draw in the circle a picture of your face that reflects your feelings at that moment.

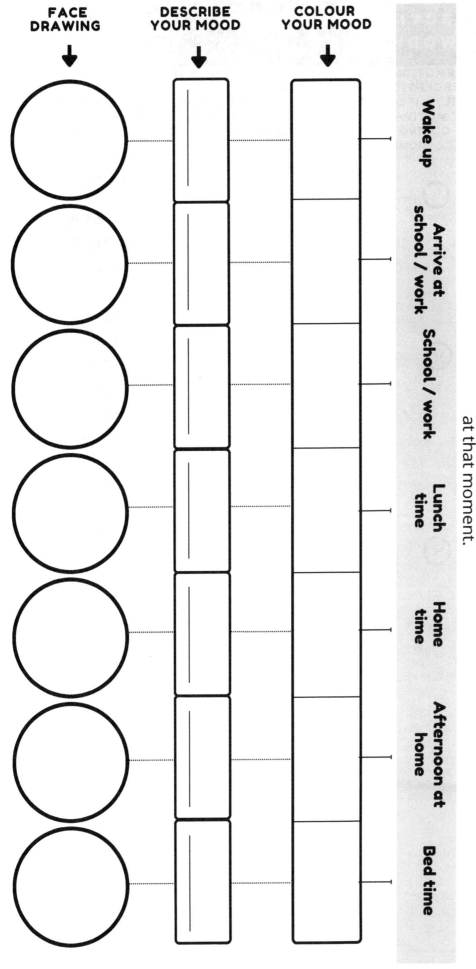

FACE DRAWING

DESCRIBE YOUR MOOD

COLOUR YOUR MOOD

Wake up

Arrive at school / work

School / work

Lunch time

Home time

Afternoon at home

Bed time

SCHIZOAFFECTIVE DISORDER
DBT WORKSHEET

TRACK PSYCHOLOGICAL AND EMOTIONAL ISSUES RELATED TO UNUSUAL
FEELINGS, PERCEPTIONS, AND ACTIONS
YOUR PROBLEMS MANAGING DAILY LIFE ACTIVITIES OR ANY DISORGANIZED
THOUGHTS DUE TO LACK OF MOTIVATION OR EMOTIONAL DRYNESS...
YOUR EMOTIONAL PROBLEMS COPING WITH CHALLENGES AT WORK, OR
HOME.

✓ ___ : ___

_____

_____

_____

✓ ___ : ___

_____

_____

_____

✓ ___ : ___

_____

_____

_____

_____

A DAILY WIN

_____

_____

_____

_____

Daily Mood Checker ✓

Mood	
ANGRY	☐
ANNOYED	☐
ANXIOUS	☐
ASHAMED	☐
AWKWARD	☐
BRAVE	☐
CALM	☐
CHEERFUL	☐
CHILL	☐
CONFUSED	☐
DISCOURAGED	☐
DISTRACTED	☐
EMBARRASSED	☐
EXCITED	☐
FRIENDLY	☐
GUILTY	☐
HAPPY	☐
HOPEFUL	☐
LONELY	☐
LOVED	☐
NERVOUS	☐
OFFENDED	☐
SCARED	☐
THOUGHTFUL	☐
TIRED	☐
UNCOMFORTABLE	☐
UNSURE	☐

DATE :   /   /

SELF-EXPOSURE
THERAPY
FOR SZA-BIPOLAR TRAITS

As part of your daily life, try to avoid situations that trigger symptoms of bipolar disorder and depression, as well as your feelings and mood swings.
But if the opposite happens, try to explore your inner triggers and contradictions in order to better understand your condition.

ALL ABOUT PSYCHOTIC AND MANIC TRIGGERS :	Notes :
	○ ○ ○ ○ ○
ALL ABOUT DEPRESSIVE TRIGGERS :	Notes :
	○ ○ ○ ○ ○
ALL ABOUT MOOD SWINGS TRIGGERS :	Notes :
	○ ○ ○ ○ ○

Notes

....

....

OVERCOMING SZA
COPING SKILLS WORKSHEET

Through this table, here are some of the problems that the majority of those suffering from schizoaffective disorder suffer from. Try to identify the difficulties associated with the items listed in the table. Try to find field solutions for them in reality, and then evaluate your progress each time.

• solving problems • forming relationships • learning useful behaviors • learn new skills	situations you exposed to and coping skills used
	👍 WHAT WAS SO COOL: 🖐 WHAT WASN'T COOL:

CHALLENGING S.Z.A SYMPTOMS DBT WORKSHEET

Date : _____

OPEN CHALLENGE

Try to develop short or long-term plans to improve the quality of your life, in which you discuss the following:

- Your Strategies to develop a support network of family , friend, and healthcare professionals to help you stay well.
- What steps can you take to manage future episodes ?
- Your ways to fix emotional , behavioral , physical changes, do you notice when you are becoming symptomatic.
- Your self-care activities and self-talk affirmations that you practice on a daily basis to improve your mood and emotional and mental health.
- Discuss anything related to your mental health, social status, and all your internal contradictions

_____

_____

_____

_____

_____

_____

_____

_____

_____

_____

_____

_____

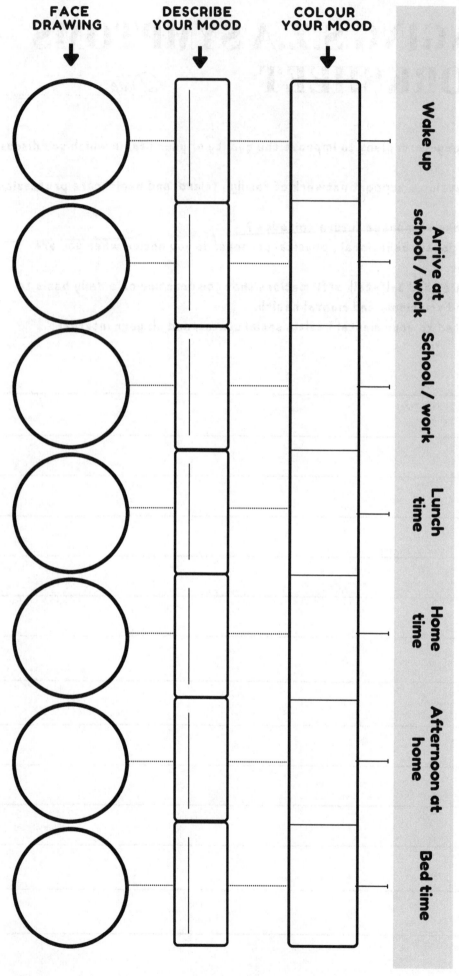

S.Z.A MOOD CYCLE

Instructions: Think about your day from start to finish. Color the first square to express your feelings each time of the day. Next, write a word that reflects your feelings, and draw in the circle a picture of your face that reflects your feelings at that moment.

FACE DRAWING

DESCRIBE YOUR MOOD

COLOUR YOUR MOOD

Wake up

Arrive at school / work

School / work

Lunch time

Home time

Afternoon at home

Bed time

SCHIZOAFFECTIVE DISORDER
DBT WORKSHEET

TRACK PSYCHOLOGICAL AND EMOTIONAL ISSUES RELATED TO UNUSUAL
FEELINGS, PERCEPTIONS, AND ACTIONS
YOUR PROBLEMS MANAGING DAILY LIFE ACTIVITIES OR ANY DISORGANIZED
THOUGHTS DUE TO LACK OF MOTIVATION OR EMOTIONAL DRYNESS...
YOUR EMOTIONAL PROBLEMS COPING WITH CHALLENGES AT WORK, OR
HOME.

✓ ___ : ___

_____

_____

_____

✓ ___ : ___

_____

_____

_____

✓ ___ : ___

_____

_____

_____

A DAILY WIN

_____

_____

_____

_____

Daily Mood Checker ✓

Mood	
ANGRY	☐
ANNOYED	☐
ANXIOUS	☐
ASHAMED	☐
AWKWARD	☐
BRAVE	☐
CALM	☐
CHEERFUL	☐
CHILL	☐
CONFUSED	☐
DISCOURAGED	☐
DISTRACTED	☐
EMBARRASSED	☐
EXCITED	☐
FRIENDLY	☐
GUILTY	☐
HAPPY	☐
HOPEFUL	☐
LONELY	☐
LOVED	☐
NERVOUS	☐
OFFENDED	☐
SCARED	☐
THOUGHTFUL	☐
TIRED	☐
UNCOMFORTABLE	☐
UNSURE	☐

SELF-EXPOSURE THERAPY FOR SZA-BIPOLAR TRAITS

As part of your daily life, try to avoid situations that trigger symptoms of bipolar disorder and depression, as well as your feelings and mood swings.
But if the opposite happens, try to explore your inner triggers and contradictions in order to better understand your condition.

ALL ABOUT PSYCHOTIC AND MANIC TRIGGERS :	Notes :
	○ ○ ○ ○ ○
ALL ABOUT DEPRESSIVE TRIGGERS :	Notes :
	○ ○ ○ ○ ○
ALL ABOUT MOOD SWINGS TRIGGERS :	Notes :
	○ ○ ○ ○ ○

Notes

....

....

OVERCOMING SZA
COPING SKILLS WORKSHEET

Through this table, here are some of the problems that the majority of those suffering from schizoaffective disorder suffer from. Try to identify the difficulties associated with the items listed in the table. Try to find field solutions for them in reality, and then evaluate your progress each time.

• solving problems • forming relationships • learning useful behaviors • learn new skills	situations you exposed to and coping skills used
	👍 **WHAT WAS SO COOL:** ✋ **WHAT WASN'T COOL:**

CHALLENGING S.Z.A SYMPTOMS DBT WORKSHEET

Date : ....

OPEN CHALLENGE

Try to develop short or long-term plans to improve the quality of your life, in which you discuss the following:

- Your Strategies to develop a support network of family , friend, and healthcare professionals to help you stay well.
- What steps can you take to manage future episodes ?
- Your ways to fix emotional , behavioral , physical changes, do you notice when you are becoming symptomatic.
- Your self-care activities and self-talk affirmations that you practice on a daily basis to improve your mood and emotional and mental health.
- Discuss anything related to your mental health, social status, and all your internal contradictions

_____

_____

_____

_____

_____

_____

_____

_____

_____

_____

_____

_____

_____

S.Z.A MOOD CYCLE

Instructions: Think about your day from start to finish. Color the first square to express your feelings each time of the day. Next, write a word that reflects your feelings, and draw in the circle a picture of your face that reflects your feelings at that moment.

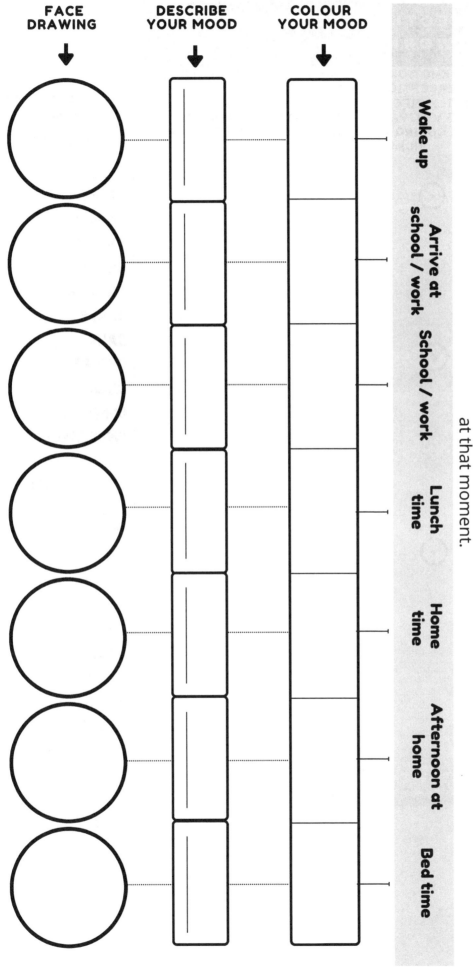

FACE DRAWING	DESCRIBE YOUR MOOD	COLOUR YOUR MOOD	
			Wake up
			Arrive at school / work
			School / work
			Lunch time
			Home time
			Afternoon at home
			Bed time

SCHIZOAFFECTIVE DISORDER DBT WORKSHEET

TRACK PSYCHOLOGICAL AND EMOTIONAL ISSUES RELATED TO UNUSUAL FEELINGS, PERCEPTIONS, AND ACTIONS
YOUR PROBLEMS MANAGING DAILY LIFE ACTIVITIES OR ANY DISORGANIZED THOUGHTS DUE TO LACK OF MOTIVATION OR EMOTIONAL DRYNESS...
YOUR EMOTIONAL PROBLEMS COPING WITH CHALLENGES AT WORK, OR HOME.

✓ __ : __

✓ __ : __

✓ __ : __

A DAILY WIN

Daily Mood Checker ✓

ANGRY	☐
ANNOYED	☐
ANXIOUS	☐
ASHAMED	☐
AWKWARD	☐
BRAVE	☐
CALM	☐
CHEERFUL	☐
CHILL	☐
CONFUSED	☐
DISCOURAGED	☐
DISTRACTED	☐
EMBARRASSED	☐
EXCITED	☐
FRIENDLY	☐
GUILTY	☐
HAPPY	☐
HOPEFUL	☐
LONELY	☐
LOVED	☐
NERVOUS	☐
OFFENDED	☐
SCARED	☐
THOUGHTFUL	☐
TIRED	☐
UNCOMFORTABLE	☐
UNSURE	☐

DATE :   /   /

SELF-EXPOSURE
THERAPY
FOR SZA-BIPOLAR TRAITS

As part of your daily life, try to avoid situations that trigger symptoms of bipolar disorder and depression, as well as your feelings and mood swings.
But if the opposite happens, try to explore your inner triggers and contradictions in order to better understand your condition.

ALL ABOUT PSYCHOTIC AND MANIC TRIGGERS :	Notes :
	◯ ◯ ◯ ◯ ◯
ALL ABOUT DEPRESSIVE TRIGGERS :	Notes :
	◯ ◯ ◯ ◯ ◯
ALL ABOUT MOOD SWINGS TRIGGERS :	Notes :
	◯ ◯ ◯ ◯ ◯

Notes

....

....

OVERCOMING SZA
COPING SKILLS WORKSHEET

Through this table, here are some of the problems that the majority of those suffering from schizoaffective disorder suffer from. Try to identify the difficulties associated with the items listed in the table. Try to find field solutions for them in reality, and then evaluate your progress each time.

• solving problems • forming relationships • learning useful behaviors • learn new skills	situations you exposed to and coping skills used
	👍 WHAT WAS SO COOL: ✋ WHAT WASN'T COOL:

CHALLENGING S.Z.A SYMPTOMS DBT WORKSHEET

Date : ....

OPEN CHALLENGE

Try to develop short or long-term plans to improve the quality of your life, in which you discuss the following:

- Your Strategies to develop a support network of family , friend, and healthcare professionals to help you stay well.
- What steps can you take to manage future episodes ?
- Your ways to fix emotional , behavioral , physical changes, do you notice when you are becoming symptomatic.
- Your self-care activities and self-talk affirmations that you practice on a daily basis to improve your mood and emotional and mental health.
- Discuss anything related to your mental health, social status, and all your internal contradictions

_____

_____

_____

_____

_____

_____

_____

_____

_____

_____

_____

S.Z.A MOOD CYCLE

Instructions: Think about your day from start to finish. Color the first square to express your feelings each time of the day. Next, write a word that reflects your feelings, and draw in the circle a picture of your face that reflects your feelings at that moment.

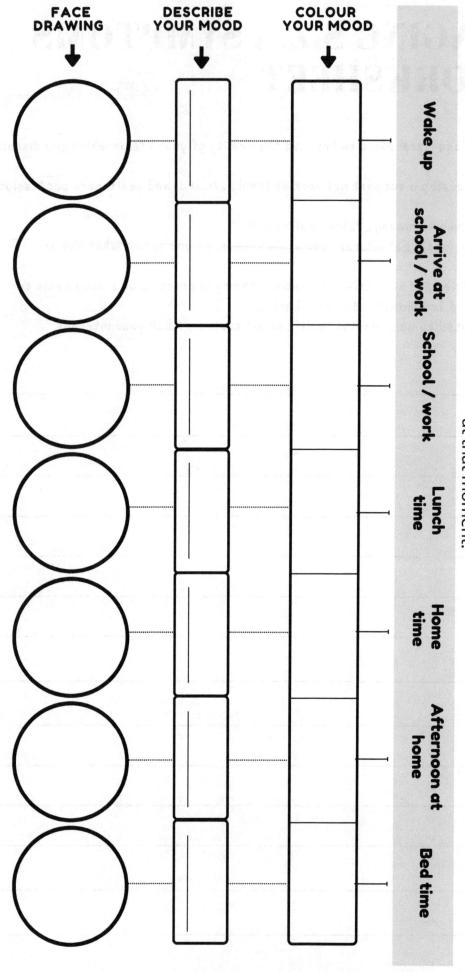

FACE DRAWING

DESCRIBE YOUR MOOD

COLOUR YOUR MOOD

Wake up

Arrive at school / work

School / work

Lunch time

Home time

Afternoon at home

Bed time

SCHIZOAFFECTIVE DISORDER
DBT WORKSHEET

TRACK PSYCHOLOGICAL AND EMOTIONAL ISSUES RELATED TO UNUSUAL
FEELINGS, PERCEPTIONS, AND ACTIONS
YOUR PROBLEMS MANAGING DAILY LIFE ACTIVITIES OR ANY DISORGANIZED
THOUGHTS DUE TO LACK OF MOTIVATION OR EMOTIONAL DRYNESS...
YOUR EMOTIONAL PROBLEMS COPING WITH CHALLENGES AT WORK, OR
HOME.

✓ ___ : ___

✓ ___ : ___

✓ ___ : ___

A DAILY WIN

Daily Mood Checker ✓	
ANGRY	☐
ANNOYED	☐
ANXIOUS	☐
ASHAMED	☐
AWKWARD	☐
BRAVE	☐
CALM	☐
CHEERFUL	☐
CHILL	☐
CONFUSED	☐
DISCOURAGED	☐
DISTRACTED	☐
EMBARRASSED	☐
EXCITED	☐
FRIENDLY	☐
GUILTY	☐
HAPPY	☐
HOPEFUL	☐
LONELY	☐
LOVED	☐
NERVOUS	☐
OFFENDED	☐
SCARED	☐
THOUGHTFUL	☐
TIRED	☐
UNCOMFORTABLE	☐
UNSURE	☐

DATE :   /   /

SELF-EXPOSURE THERAPY FOR SZA-BIPOLAR TRAITS

As part of your daily life, try to avoid situations that trigger symptoms of bipolar disorder and depression, as well as your feelings and mood swings.
But if the opposite happens, try to explore your inner triggers and contradictions in order to better understand your condition.

ALL ABOUT PSYCHOTIC AND MANIC TRIGGERS :	Notes :
	⃝ ⃝ ⃝ ⃝ ⃝
ALL ABOUT DEPRESSIVE TRIGGERS :	Notes :
	⃝ ⃝ ⃝ ⃝ ⃝
ALL ABOUT MOOD SWINGS TRIGGERS :	Notes :
	⃝ ⃝ ⃝ ⃝ ⃝

Notes

....

....

OVERCOMING SZA
COPING SKILLS WORKSHEET

Through this table, here are some of the problems that the majority of those suffering from schizoaffective disorder suffer from. Try to identify the difficulties associated with the items listed in the table. Try to find field solutions for them in reality, and then evaluate your progress each time.

• solving problems • forming relationships • learning useful behaviors • learn new skills	situations you exposed to and coping skills used
	👍 **WHAT WAS SO COOL:** ✋ **WHAT WASN'T COOL:**

CHALLENGING S.Z.A SYMPTOMS DBT WORKSHEET

Date : ....

OPEN CHALLENGE

Try to develop short or long-term plans to improve the quality of your life, in which you discuss the following:

- Your Strategies to develop a support network of family , friend, and healthcare professionals to help you stay well.
- What steps can you take to manage future episodes ?
- Your ways to fix emotional , behavioral , physical changes, do you notice when you are becoming symptomatic.
- Your self-care activities and self-talk affirmations that you practice on a daily basis to improve your mood and emotional and mental health.
- Discuss anything related to your mental health, social status, and all your internal contradictions

_____

_____

_____

_____

_____

_____

_____

_____

_____

_____

_____

_____

_____

_____

S.Z.A MOOD CYCLE

Instructions: Think about your day from start to finish. Color the first square to express your feelings each time of the day. Next, write a word that reflects your feelings, and draw in the circle a picture of your face that reflects your feelings at that moment.

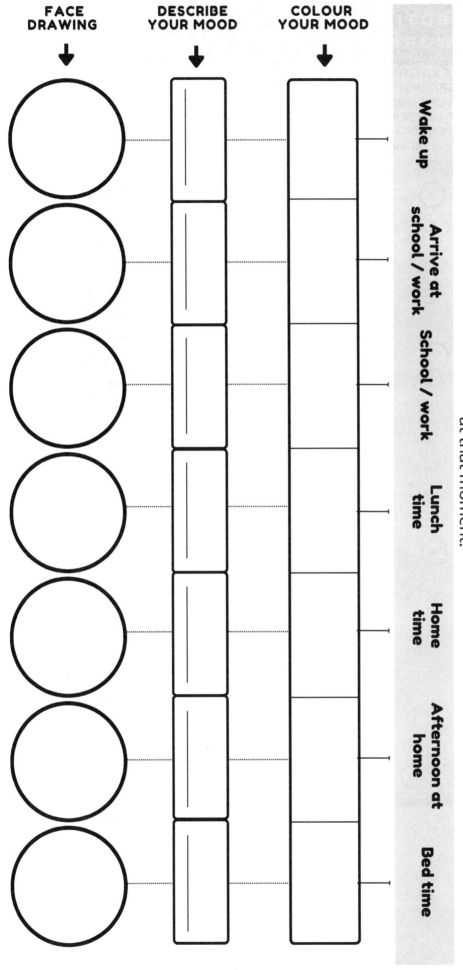

FACE DRAWING

DESCRIBE YOUR MOOD

COLOUR YOUR MOOD

Wake up

Arrive at school / work

School / work

Lunch time

Home time

Afternoon at home

Bed time

SCHIZOAFFECTIVE DISORDER
DBT WORKSHEET

Date : / /

Sleep quality :

TRACK PSYCHOLOGICAL AND EMOTIONAL ISSUES RELATED TO UNUSUAL
FEELINGS, PERCEPTIONS, AND ACTIONS
YOUR PROBLEMS MANAGING DAILY LIFE ACTIVITIES OR ANY DISORGANIZED
THOUGHTS DUE TO LACK OF MOTIVATION OR EMOTIONAL DRYNESS...
YOUR EMOTIONAL PROBLEMS COPING WITH CHALLENGES AT WORK, OR
HOME.

✓ ___ : ___

✓ ___ : ___

✓ ___ : ___

A DAILY WIN

Daily Mood Checker ✓

ANGRY	☐
ANNOYED	☐
ANXIOUS	☐
ASHAMED	☐
AWKWARD	☐
BRAVE	☐
CALM	☐
CHEERFUL	☐
CHILL	☐
CONFUSED	☐
DISCOURAGED	☐
DISTRACTED	☐
EMBARRASSED	☐
EXCITED	☐
FRIENDLY	☐
GUILTY	☐
HAPPY	☐
HOPEFUL	☐
LONELY	☐
LOVED	☐
NERVOUS	☐
OFFENDED	☐
SCARED	☐
THOUGHTFUL	☐
TIRED	☐
UNCOMFORTABLE	☐
UNSURE	☐

DATE : / /

SELF-EXPOSURE THERAPY FOR SZA-BIPOLAR TRAITS

As part of your daily life, try to avoid situations that trigger symptoms of bipolar disorder and depression, as well as your feelings and mood swings.

But if the opposite happens, try to explore your inner triggers and contradictions in order to better understand your condition.

ALL ABOUT PSYCHOTIC AND MANIC TRIGGERS :	Notes :
	○ ○ ○ ○ ○
ALL ABOUT DEPRESSIVE TRIGGERS :	Notes :
	○ ○ ○ ○ ○
ALL ABOUT MOOD SWINGS TRIGGERS :	Notes :
	○ ○ ○ ○ ○

Notes

....

....

OVERCOMING SZA
COPING SKILLS WORKSHEET

Through this table, here are some of the problems that the majority of those suffering from schizoaffective disorder suffer from. Try to identify the difficulties associated with the items listed in the table. Try to find field solutions for them in reality, and then evaluate your progress each time.

• solving problems • forming relationships • learning useful behaviors • learn new skills	situations you exposed to and coping skills used
	👍 **WHAT WAS SO COOL:** ✋ **WHAT WASN'T COOL:**

CHALLENGING S.Z.A SYMPTOMS DBT WORKSHEET

Date : ....

OPEN CHALLENGE

Try to develop short or long-term plans to improve the quality of your life, in which you discuss the following:

- Your Strategies to develop a support network of family , friend, and healthcare professionals to help you stay well.
- What steps can you take to manage future episodes ?
- Your ways to fix emotional , behavioral , physical changes, do you notice when you are becoming symptomatic.
- Your self-care activities and self-talk affirmations that you practice on a daily basis to improve your mood and emotional and mental health.
- Discuss anything related to your mental health, social status, and all your internal contradictions

_____

_____

_____

_____

_____

_____

_____

_____

_____

_____

_____

_____

S.Z.A MOOD CYCLE

Instructions: Think about your day from start to finish. Color the first square to express your feelings each time of the day. Next, write a word that reflects your feelings, and draw in the circle a picture of your face that reflects your feelings at that moment.

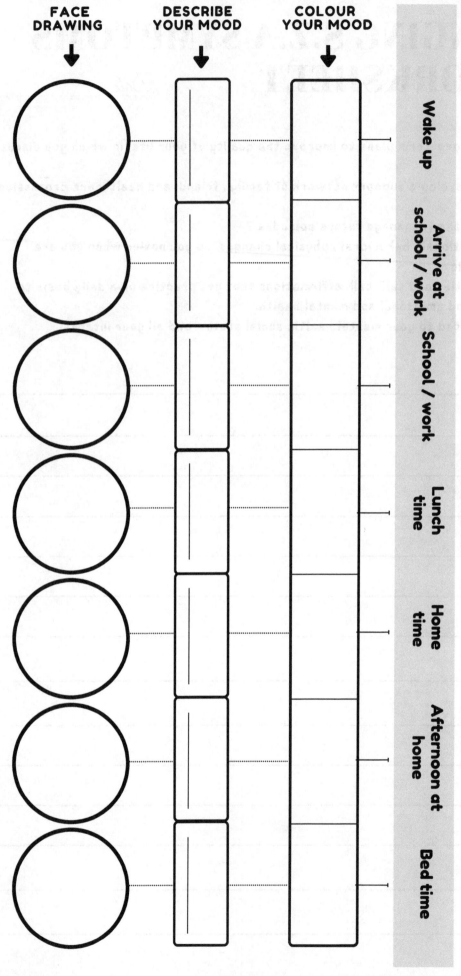

FACE DRAWING

DESCRIBE YOUR MOOD

COLOUR YOUR MOOD

Wake up

Arrive at school / work

School / work

Lunch time

Home time

Afternoon at home

Bed time

SCHIZOAFFECTIVE DISORDER DBT WORKSHEET

TRACK PSYCHOLOGICAL AND EMOTIONAL ISSUES RELATED TO UNUSUAL FEELINGS, PERCEPTIONS, AND ACTIONS
YOUR PROBLEMS MANAGING DAILY LIFE ACTIVITIES OR ANY DISORGANIZED THOUGHTS DUE TO LACK OF MOTIVATION OR EMOTIONAL DRYNESS...
YOUR EMOTIONAL PROBLEMS COPING WITH CHALLENGES AT WORK, OR HOME.

✓ ___ : ___

✓ ___ : ___

✓ ___ : ___

A DAILY WIN

Daily Mood Checker ✓

Mood	
ANGRY	☐
ANNOYED	☐
ANXIOUS	☐
ASHAMED	☐
AWKWARD	☐
BRAVE	☐
CALM	☐
CHEERFUL	☐
CHILL	☐
CONFUSED	☐
DISCOURAGED	☐
DISTRACTED	☐
EMBARRASSED	☐
EXCITED	☐
FRIENDLY	☐
GUILTY	☐
HAPPY	☐
HOPEFUL	☐
LONELY	☐
LOVED	☐
NERVOUS	☐
OFFENDED	☐
SCARED	☐
THOUGHTFUL	☐
TIRED	☐
UNCOMFORTABLE	☐
UNSURE	☐

DATE :   /   /

SELF-EXPOSURE THERAPY FOR SZA-BIPOLAR TRAITS

As part of your daily life, try to avoid situations that trigger symptoms of bipolar disorder and depression, as well as your feelings and mood swings.
But if the opposite happens, try to explore your inner triggers and contradictions in order to better understand your condition.

ALL ABOUT PSYCHOTIC AND MANIC TRIGGERS :	Notes :
	○ ○ ○ ○ ○
ALL ABOUT DEPRESSIVE TRIGGERS :	Notes :
	○ ○ ○ ○ ○
ALL ABOUT MOOD SWINGS TRIGGERS :	Notes :
	○ ○ ○ ○ ○

Notes

....

....

OVERCOMING SZA
COPING SKILLS WORKSHEET

Through this table, here are some of the problems that the majority of those suffering from schizoaffective disorder suffer from. Try to identify the difficulties associated with the items listed in the table. Try to find field solutions for them in reality, and then evaluate your progress each time.

• solving problems • forming relationships • learning useful behaviors • learn new skills	situations you exposed to and coping skills used
	👍 **WHAT WAS SO COOL:** ✋ **WHAT WASN'T COOL:**

CHALLENGING S.Z.A SYMPTOMS DBT WORKSHEET

Date : ....

Try to develop short or long-term plans to improve the quality of your life, in which you discuss the following:

- Your Strategies to develop a support network of family , friend, and healthcare professionals to help you stay well.
- What steps can you take to manage future episodes ?
- Your ways to fix emotional , behavioral , physical changes, do you notice when you are becoming symptomatic.
- Your self-care activities and self-talk affirmations that you practice on a daily basis to improve your mood and emotional and mental health.
- Discuss anything related to your mental health, social status, and all your internal contradictions

_____

_____

_____

_____

_____

_____

_____

_____

_____

_____

_____

_____

_____

_____

S.Z.A MOOD CYCLE

Instructions: Think about your day from start to finish. Color the first square to express your feelings each time of the day. Next, write a word that reflects your feelings, and draw in the circle a picture of your face that reflects your feelings at that moment.

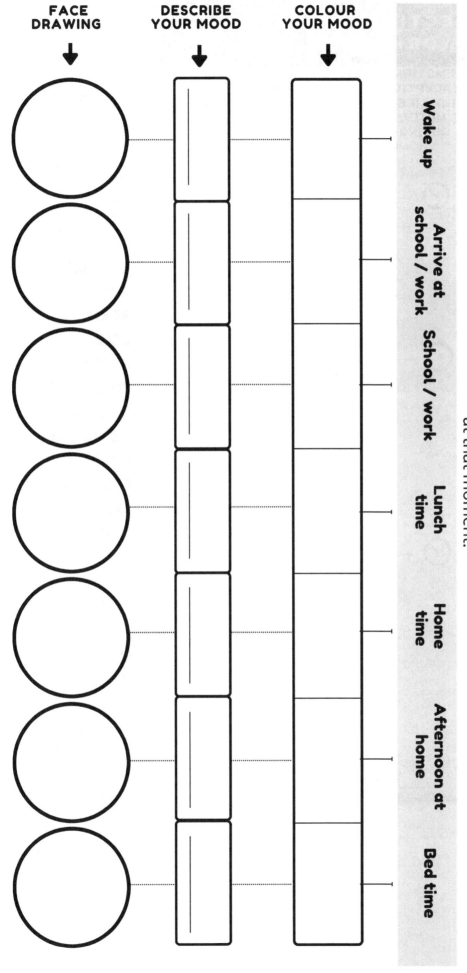

FACE DRAWING

DESCRIBE YOUR MOOD

COLOUR YOUR MOOD

Wake up

Arrive at school / work

School / work

Lunch time

Home time

Afternoon at home

Bed time

SCHIZOAFFECTIVE DISORDER
DBT WORKSHEET

Date : / /

Sleep quality :

TRACK PSYCHOLOGICAL AND EMOTIONAL ISSUES RELATED TO UNUSUAL FEELINGS, PERCEPTIONS, AND ACTIONS
YOUR PROBLEMS MANAGING DAILY LIFE ACTIVITIES OR ANY DISORGANIZED THOUGHTS DUE TO LACK OF MOTIVATION OR EMOTIONAL DRYNESS...
YOUR EMOTIONAL PROBLEMS COPING WITH CHALLENGES AT WORK, OR HOME.

✓ __ : __

✓ __ : __

✓ __ : __

A DAILY WIN

Daily Mood Checker ✓

ANGRY	☐
ANNOYED	☐
ANXIOUS	☐
ASHAMED	☐
AWKWARD	☐
BRAVE	☐
CALM	☐
CHEERFUL	☐
CHILL	☐
CONFUSED	☐
DISCOURAGED	☐
DISTRACTED	☐
EMBARRASSED	☐
EXCITED	☐
FRIENDLY	☐
GUILTY	☐
HAPPY	☐
HOPEFUL	☐
LONELY	☐
LOVED	☐
NERVOUS	☐
OFFENDED	☐
SCARED	☐
THOUGHTFUL	☐
TIRED	☐
UNCOMFORTABLE	☐
UNSURE	☐

RATE YOUR PSYCHOLOGICAL SATISFACTION : ... **/10**

SELF-EXPOSURE THERAPY FOR SZA-BIPOLAR TRAITS

As part of your daily life, try to avoid situations that trigger symptoms of bipolar disorder and depression, as well as your feelings and mood swings.
But if the opposite happens, try to explore your inner triggers and contradictions in order to better understand your condition.

ALL ABOUT PSYCHOTIC AND MANIC TRIGGERS :	Notes :
	○ ○ ○ ○ ○
ALL ABOUT DEPRESSIVE TRIGGERS : *Notes :*	
	○ ○ ○ ○ ○
ALL ABOUT MOOD SWINGS TRIGGERS :	Notes :
	○ ○ ○ ○ ○

Notes

....

....

OVERCOMING SZA
COPING SKILLS WORKSHEET

Through this table, here are some of the problems that the majority of those suffering from schizoaffective disorder suffer from. Try to identify the difficulties associated with the items listed in the table. Try to find field solutions for them in reality, and then evaluate your progress each time.

• solving problems • forming relationships • learning useful behaviors • learn new skills	situations you exposed to and coping skills used
	👍 WHAT WAS SO COOL: ✋ WHAT WASN'T COOL:

CHALLENGING S.Z.A SYMPTOMS DBT WORKSHEET

Date : ....

OPEN CHALLENGE

Try to develop short or long-term plans to improve the quality of your life, in which you discuss the following:

- Your Strategies to develop a support network of family , friend, and healthcare professionals to help you stay well.
- What steps can you take to manage future episodes ?
- Your ways to fix emotional , behavioral , physical changes, do you notice when you are becoming symptomatic.
- Your self-care activities and self-talk affirmations that you practice on a daily basis to improve your mood and emotional and mental health.
- Discuss anything related to your mental health, social status, and all your internal contradictions

_____

_____

_____

_____

_____

_____

_____

_____

_____

_____

_____

_____

S.Z.A MOOD CYCLE

Instructions: Think about your day from start to finish. Color the first square to express your feelings each time of the day. Next, write a word that reflects your feelings, and draw in the circle a picture of your face that reflects your feelings at that moment.

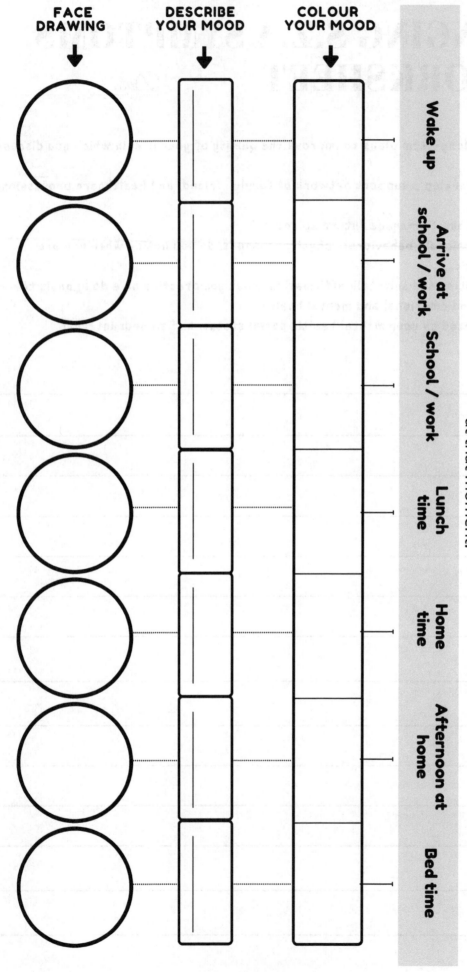

FACE DRAWING

DESCRIBE YOUR MOOD

COLOUR YOUR MOOD

Wake up

Arrive at school / work

School / work

Lunch time

Home time

Afternoon at home

Bed time

SCHIZOAFFECTIVE DISORDER DBT WORKSHEET

TRACK PSYCHOLOGICAL AND EMOTIONAL ISSUES RELATED TO UNUSUAL FEELINGS, PERCEPTIONS, AND ACTIONS
YOUR PROBLEMS MANAGING DAILY LIFE ACTIVITIES OR ANY DISORGANIZED THOUGHTS DUE TO LACK OF MOTIVATION OR EMOTIONAL DRYNESS...
YOUR EMOTIONAL PROBLEMS COPING WITH CHALLENGES AT WORK, OR HOME.

✓ __ : __

_____

_____

_____

✓ __ : __

_____

_____

_____

✓ __ : __

_____

_____

_____

A DAILY WIN

_____

_____

_____

Daily Mood Checker ✓

ANGRY	☐
ANNOYED	☐
ANXIOUS	☐
ASHAMED	☐
AWKWARD	☐
BRAVE	☐
CALM	☐
CHEERFUL	☐
CHILL	☐
CONFUSED	☐
DISCOURAGED	☐
DISTRACTED	☐
EMBARRASSED	☐
EXCITED	☐
FRIENDLY	☐
GUILTY	☐
HAPPY	☐
HOPEFUL	☐
LONELY	☐
LOVED	☐
NERVOUS	☐
OFFENDED	☐
SCARED	☐
THOUGHTFUL	☐
TIRED	☐
UNCOMFORTABLE	☐
UNSURE	☐

DATE :   /   /

SELF-EXPOSURE THERAPY FOR SZA-BIPOLAR TRAITS

As part of your daily life, try to avoid situations that trigger symptoms of bipolar disorder and depression, as well as your feelings and mood swings.
But if the opposite happens, try to explore your inner triggers and contradictions in order to better understand your condition.

ALL ABOUT PSYCHOTIC AND MANIC TRIGGERS :	Notes :
	○ ○ ○ ○ ○
ALL ABOUT DEPRESSIVE TRIGGERS :	Notes :
	○ ○ ○ ○ ○
ALL ABOUT MOOD SWINGS TRIGGERS :	Notes :
	○ ○ ○ ○ ○

Notes

....

....

OVERCOMING SZA
COPING SKILLS WORKSHEET

Through this table, here are some of the problems that the majority of those suffering from schizoaffective disorder suffer from. Try to identify the difficulties associated with the items listed in the table. Try to find field solutions for them in reality, and then evaluate your progress each time.

• solving problems • forming relationships • learning useful behaviors • learn new skills	situations you exposed to and coping skills used
	👍 **WHAT WAS SO COOL:** ✋ **WHAT WASN'T COOL:**

CHALLENGING S.Z.A SYMPTOMS
DBT WORKSHEET

Date : ....

OPEN CHALLENGE

Try to develop short or long-term plans to improve the quality of your life, in which you discuss the following:

- Your Strategies to develop a support network of family , friend, and healthcare professionals to help you stay well.
- What steps can you take to manage future episodes ?
- Your ways to fix emotional , behavioral , physical changes, do you notice when you are becoming symptomatic.
- Your self-care activities and self-talk affirmations that you practice on a daily basis to improve your mood and emotional and mental health.
- Discuss anything related to your mental health, social status, and all your internal contradictions

_____

_____

_____

_____

_____

_____

_____

_____

_____

_____

_____

_____

S.Z.A MOOD CYCLE

Instructions: Think about your day from start to finish. Color the first square to express your feelings each time of the day. Next, write a word that reflects your feelings, and draw in the circle a picture of your face that reflects your feelings at that moment.

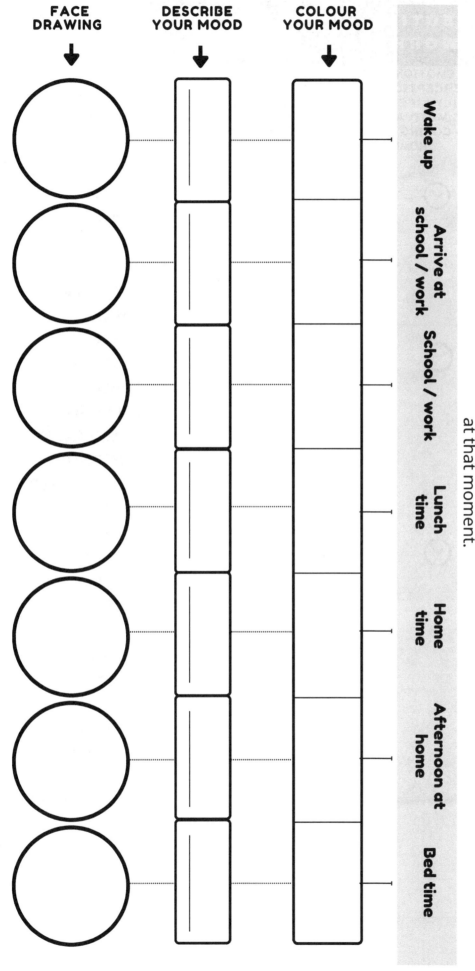

FACE DRAWING

DESCRIBE YOUR MOOD

COLOUR YOUR MOOD

Wake up

Arrive at school / work

School / work

Lunch time

Home time

Afternoon at home

Bed time

SCHIZOAFFECTIVE DISORDER
DBT WORKSHEET

TRACK PSYCHOLOGICAL AND EMOTIONAL ISSUES RELATED TO UNUSUAL FEELINGS, PERCEPTIONS, AND ACTIONS
YOUR PROBLEMS MANAGING DAILY LIFE ACTIVITIES OR ANY DISORGANIZED THOUGHTS DUE TO LACK OF MOTIVATION OR EMOTIONAL DRYNESS...
YOUR EMOTIONAL PROBLEMS COPING WITH CHALLENGES AT WORK, OR HOME.

✓ ___ : ___

✓ ___ : ___

✓ ___ : ___

A DAILY WIN

Daily Mood Checker ✓

ANGRY	☐
ANNOYED	☐
ANXIOUS	☐
ASHAMED	☐
AWKWARD	☐
BRAVE	☐
CALM	☐
CHEERFUL	☐
CHILL	☐
CONFUSED	☐
DISCOURAGED	☐
DISTRACTED	☐
EMBARRASSED	☐
EXCITED	☐
FRIENDLY	☐
GUILTY	☐
HAPPY	☐
HOPEFUL	☐
LONELY	☐
LOVED	☐
NERVOUS	☐
OFFENDED	☐
SCARED	☐
THOUGHTFUL	☐
TIRED	☐
UNCOMFORTABLE	☐
UNSURE	☐

DATE :   /   /

SELF-EXPOSURE
THERAPY
FOR SZA-BIPOLAR TRAITS

As part of your daily life, try to avoid situations that trigger symptoms of bipolar disorder and depression, as well as your feelings and mood swings.
But if the opposite happens, try to explore your inner triggers and contradictions in order to better understand your condition.

ALL ABOUT PSYCHOTIC AND MANIC TRIGGERS :	Notes :
	○ ○ ○ ○ ○
ALL ABOUT DEPRESSIVE TRIGGERS :	Notes :
	○ ○ ○ ○ ○
ALL ABOUT MOOD SWINGS TRIGGERS :	Notes :
	○ ○ ○ ○ ○

Notes

....

....

OVERCOMING SZA
COPING SKILLS WORKSHEET

Through this table, here are some of the problems that the majority of those suffering from schizoaffective disorder suffer from. Try to identify the difficulties associated with the items listed in the table. Try to find field solutions for them in reality, and then evaluate your progress each time.

• solving problems • forming relationships • learning useful behaviors • learn new skills	situations you exposed to and coping skills used
	👍 WHAT WAS SO COOL: ✋ WHAT WASN'T COOL:

CHALLENGING S.Z.A SYMPTOMS DBT WORKSHEET

OPEN CHALLENGE

Try to develop short or long-term plans to improve the quality of your life, in which you discuss the following:

- Your Strategies to develop a support network of family , friend, and healthcare professionals to help you stay well.
- What steps can you take to manage future episodes ?
- Your ways to fix emotional , behavioral , physical changes, do you notice when you are becoming symptomatic.
- Your self-care activities and self-talk affirmations that you practice on a daily basis to improve your mood and emotional and mental health.
- Discuss anything related to your mental health, social status, and all your internal contradictions

_____

_____

_____

_____

_____

_____

_____

_____

_____

_____

_____

_____

_____

S.Z.A MOOD CYCLE

Instructions: Think about your day from start to finish. Color the first square to express your feelings each time of the day. Next, write a word that reflects your feelings, and draw in the circle a picture of your face that reflects your feelings at that moment.

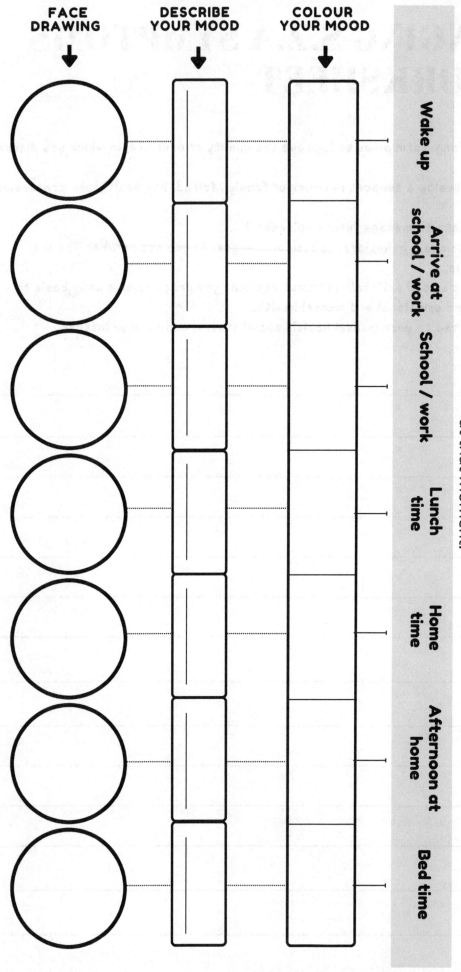

FACE DRAWING

DESCRIBE YOUR MOOD

COLOUR YOUR MOOD

Wake up

Arrive at school / work

School / work

Lunch time

Home time

Afternoon at home

Bed time

SCHIZOAFFECTIVE DISORDER DBT WORKSHEET

TRACK PSYCHOLOGICAL AND EMOTIONAL ISSUES RELATED TO UNUSUAL FEELINGS, PERCEPTIONS, AND ACTIONS
YOUR PROBLEMS MANAGING DAILY LIFE ACTIVITIES OR ANY DISORGANIZED THOUGHTS DUE TO LACK OF MOTIVATION OR EMOTIONAL DRYNESS...
YOUR EMOTIONAL PROBLEMS COPING WITH CHALLENGES AT WORK, OR HOME.

✓ __ : __

✓ __ : __

✓ __ : __

A DAILY WIN

Daily Mood Checker ✓

Mood	
ANGRY	☐
ANNOYED	☐
ANXIOUS	☐
ASHAMED	☐
AWKWARD	☐
BRAVE	☐
CALM	☐
CHEERFUL	☐
CHILL	☐
CONFUSED	☐
DISCOURAGED	☐
DISTRACTED	☐
EMBARRASSED	☐
EXCITED	☐
FRIENDLY	☐
GUILTY	☐
HAPPY	☐
HOPEFUL	☐
LONELY	☐
LOVED	☐
NERVOUS	☐
OFFENDED	☐
SCARED	☐
THOUGHTFUL	☐
TIRED	☐
UNCOMFORTABLE	☐
UNSURE	☐

DATE :   /   /

SELF-EXPOSURE THERAPY FOR SZA-BIPOLAR TRAITS

As part of your daily life, try to avoid situations that trigger symptoms of bipolar disorder and depression, as well as your feelings and mood swings.
But if the opposite happens, try to explore your inner triggers and contradictions in order to better understand your condition.

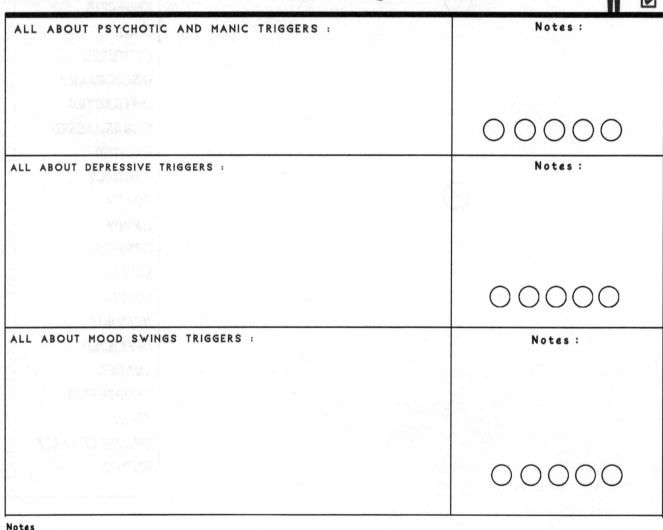

ALL ABOUT PSYCHOTIC AND MANIC TRIGGERS :	Notes :
	○ ○ ○ ○ ○

ALL ABOUT DEPRESSIVE TRIGGERS :	Notes :
	○ ○ ○ ○ ○

ALL ABOUT MOOD SWINGS TRIGGERS :	Notes :
	○ ○ ○ ○ ○

Notes

....

....

OVERCOMING SZA
COPING SKILLS WORKSHEET

Through this table, here are some of the problems that the majority of those suffering from schizoaffective disorder suffer from. Try to identify the difficulties associated with the items listed in the table. Try to find field solutions for them in reality, and then evaluate your progress each time.

• solving problems • forming relationships • learning useful behaviors • learn new skills	situations you exposed to and coping skills used
	👍 **WHAT WAS SO COOL:** ✋ **WHAT WASN'T COOL:**

CHALLENGING S.Z.A SYMPTOMS DBT WORKSHEET

Date :

OPEN CHALLENGE

Try to develop short or long-term plans to improve the quality of your life, in which you discuss the following:

- Your Strategies to develop a support network of family , friend, and healthcare professionals to help you stay well.
- What steps can you take to manage future episodes ?
- Your ways to fix emotional , behavioral , physical changes, do you notice when you are becoming symptomatic.
- Your self-care activities and self-talk affirmations that you practice on a daily basis to improve your mood and emotional and mental health.
- Discuss anything related to your mental health, social status, and all your internal contradictions

_____

_____

_____

_____

_____

_____

_____

_____

_____

_____

_____

S.Z.A MOOD CYCLE

Instructions: Think about your day from start to finish. Color the first square to express your feelings each time of the day. Next, write a word that reflects your feelings, and draw in the circle a picture of your face that reflects your feelings at that moment.

FACE DRAWING	DESCRIBE YOUR MOOD	COLOUR YOUR MOOD	
⬇	⬇	⬇	
◯			Wake up
◯			Arrive at school / work
◯			School / work
◯			Lunch time
◯			Home time
◯			Afternoon at home
◯			Bed time

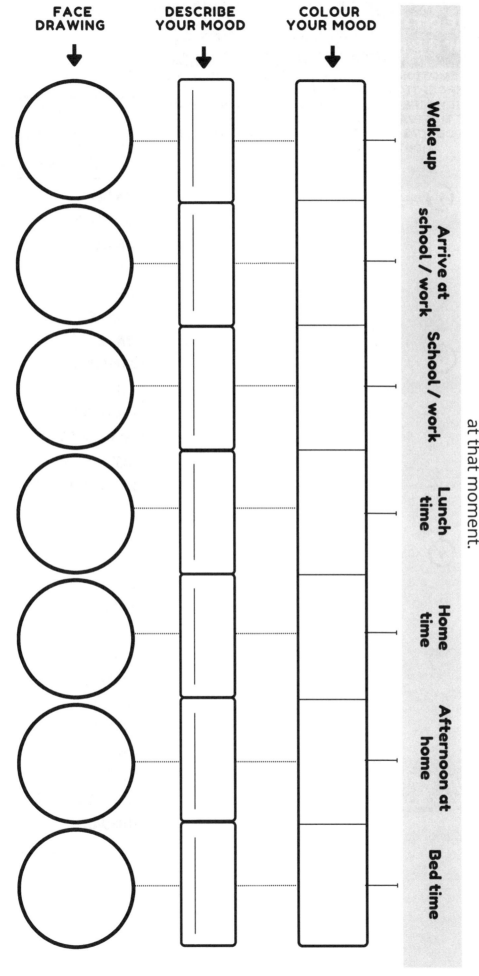

SCHIZOAFFECTIVE DISORDER
DBT WORKSHEET

TRACK PSYCHOLOGICAL AND EMOTIONAL ISSUES RELATED TO UNUSUAL
FEELINGS, PERCEPTIONS, AND ACTIONS
YOUR PROBLEMS MANAGING DAILY LIFE ACTIVITIES OR ANY DISORGANIZED
THOUGHTS DUE TO LACK OF MOTIVATION OR EMOTIONAL DRYNESS...
YOUR EMOTIONAL PROBLEMS COPING WITH CHALLENGES AT WORK, OR
HOME.

Date : / /

Sleep quality :

✓ ⊘ — : —

✓ ⊘ — : —

✓ ⊘ — : —

A DAILY WIN

Daily Mood Checker ✓

ANGRY	☐
ANNOYED	☐
ANXIOUS	☐
ASHAMED	☐
AWKWARD	☐
BRAVE	☐
CALM	☐
CHEERFUL	☐
CHILL	☐
CONFUSED	☐
DISCOURAGED	☐
DISTRACTED	☐
EMBARRASSED	☐
EXCITED	☐
FRIENDLY	☐
GUILTY	☐
HAPPY	☐
HOPEFUL	☐
LONELY	☐
LOVED	☐
NERVOUS	☐
OFFENDED	☐
SCARED	☐
THOUGHTFUL	☐
TIRED	☐
UNCOMFORTABLE	☐
UNSURE	☐

RATE YOUR PSYCHOLOGICAL SATISFACTION : ... /10

SELF-EXPOSURE THERAPY FOR SZA-BIPOLAR TRAITS

As part of your daily life, try to avoid situations that trigger symptoms of bipolar disorder and depression, as well as your feelings and mood swings.
But if the opposite happens, try to explore your inner triggers and contradictions in order to better understand your condition.

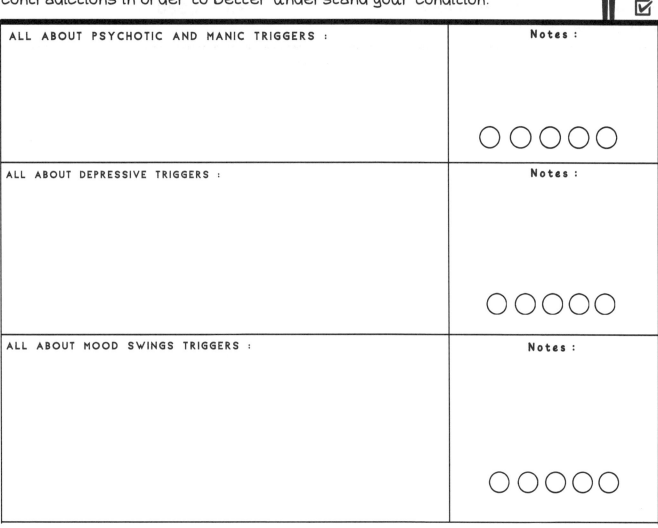

ALL ABOUT PSYCHOTIC AND MANIC TRIGGERS :

Notes :

◯ ◯ ◯ ◯ ◯

ALL ABOUT DEPRESSIVE TRIGGERS :

Notes :

◯ ◯ ◯ ◯ ◯

ALL ABOUT MOOD SWINGS TRIGGERS :

Notes :

◯ ◯ ◯ ◯ ◯

Notes

....

....

OVERCOMING SZA
COPING SKILLS WORKSHEET

Through this table, here are some of the problems that the majority of those suffering from schizoaffective disorder suffer from. Try to identify the difficulties associated with the items listed in the table. Try to find field solutions for them in reality, and then evaluate your progress each time.

• solving problems • forming relationships • learning useful behaviors • learn new skills	situations you exposed to and coping skills used
	👍 **WHAT WAS SO COOL:** ✋ **WHAT WASN'T COOL:**

CHALLENGING S.Z.A SYMPTOMS DBT WORKSHEET

Date : ....

OPEN CHALLENGE

Try to develop short or long-term plans to improve the quality of your life, in which you discuss the following:

- Your Strategies to develop a support network of family , friend, and healthcare professionals to help you stay well.
- What steps can you take to manage future episodes ?
- Your ways to fix emotional , behavioral , physical changes, do you notice when you are becoming symptomatic.
- Your self-care activities and self-talk affirmations that you practice on a daily basis to improve your mood and emotional and mental health.
- Discuss anything related to your mental health, social status, and all your internal contradictions

_____

_____

_____

_____

_____

_____

_____

_____

_____

_____

_____

_____

_____

_____

S.Z.A MOOD CYCLE

Instructions: Think about your day from start to finish. Color the first square to express your feelings each time of the day. Next, write a word that reflects your feelings, and draw in the circle a picture of your face that reflects your feelings at that moment.

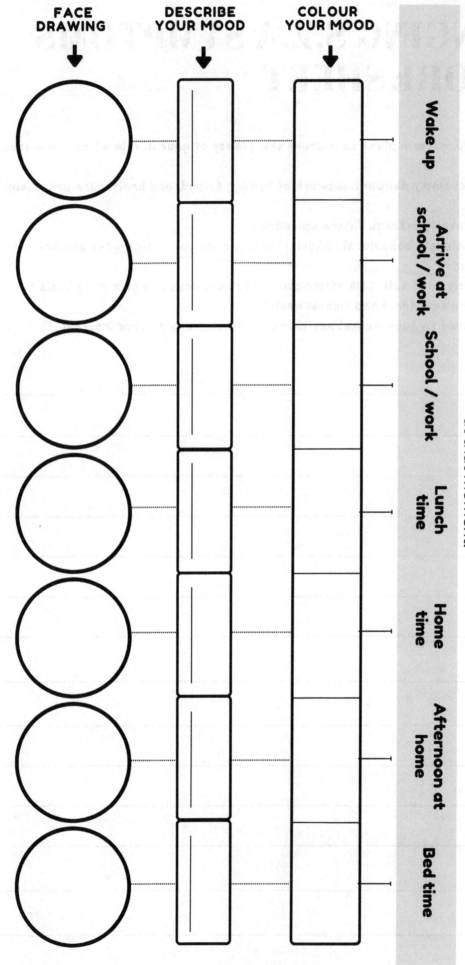

FACE DRAWING

DESCRIBE YOUR MOOD

COLOUR YOUR MOOD

Wake up

Arrive at school / work

School / work

Lunch time

Home time

Afternoon at home

Bed time

Made in United States
Troutdale, OR
07/21/2024